Some Flawed Magic

Some Flawed Magic

Poems by

Patricia Caspers

Cover design by Shay Culligan
Cover art "Red Curtain" by Paulina Swietliczko
Author photo credit: Rick Ross

ISBN: 978-1-63980-012-4

Kelsay Books
502 South 1040 East, A-119
American Fork, Utah 84003
Kelsaybooks.com

Thanks

Some Flawed Magic was twenty years in the making, written, for the most part, before my first published book was released. So many lives have inspired, so many hands have touched the words in this collection, and I'm grateful to more people than it is possible for me to name. Here are a few:

Thank you to Karen Kelsay and everyone at Kelsay Press for saying yes to this manuscript just as I was about to tuck it away in a locked cupboard forever.

Thank you to John McCarthy and Patricia Colleen Murphy for the kindest words, and to Paulina Swietliczko for her poignant artwork.

Thank you to my many beloved workshoppers, editors and cheerleaders for their kindness, insight, and support, including Lisa Ahn, Katherine Case, Renato Gasparetti, Joan Kwon Glass, Laura Grodrian, Ben Joyce, Wun Kuen, Brian Love, Annie Stenzel, Jennifer K. Sweeney, and Claire Unis.

Thank you to the Red Fox Underground Poetry Collective for its early morning kinship, including Carol Lynn Grellas, Taylor Graham, Lara Gularte, Irene Lipshin, Moira Magneson, Carol Louise Moon, Jenifer Vernon, Kate Wells, and Wendy Williams.

Thank you to La Pittura, particularly Cynthia Della Pena, Molly Dunham, and Dana Ross, for the gift of space, honest conversations, and paint on the page that flowed into text.

Thank you to the fine professors at Chico State and Mills College, including Elmaz Abinader, Chana Bloch, Carole Oles, Gary Thompson, and Elizabeth Willis. I am also grateful for Kirsten Saxton who improved my use of punctuation exponentially.

Thank you to the folx at Hedgebrook, for the gift of time, community, and delicious food.

Thank you to my husband, Rick Caspers Ross, for listening attentively to each poem, each revision, and for never complaining about the submission fees trickling out of our bank account.

Big thank yous and so much love to our children, Jacob, Olivia, and Seamus, who always keep it real.

Finally, I have more appreciation than I am able to express for my family—here, and on the other side—for their inspiration, support, and love: Terry Bryce, Martin Caspers, Patricia and James Caspers, Donna Denman, Chuck Daniels, Sandy and Gary Floyd, Dale Floyd, Mona and Henry Floyd, Ivy Jewel Myrick, Irene Stockdale VanZandt, and Norman VanZandt.

Finally, thank you, dear reader, for coming all this way with me.

Acknowledgments

I am grateful to the editors and staff of the publications where some of these poems first appeared, sometimes in previous iterations:

Atticus Review: "Narcissus Bulb"

Auburn Journal: "Re-reading the Pregnancy Book 20 Years Later"

Barnstorm: "Canyon Fire"

Barren Magazine: "風の電話"

Birdcoat Quarterly: "Bird Damage / Fire Blight"

Border Crossing: "Father As," "How It's Done"

Broome Review: "The Sewing Machine"

Catamaran: "Double Negative"

Facets Magazine: "Chico, September," "Slaughtering Days"

Limestone: "Family Portrait"

Literary Mama: "Mourning with Hummingbird," "Postcard from the Winterside of Spring"

Main Street Rag: "While Driving Highway 80, I Think of My Father"

Nimrod: "Life with Fever"

Pirene's Fountain: "Public Radio"

Quiddity: "Ode to E.B."

Rose and Thorn: "Problem Solving"

Slipstream: "A Gas Station Near Bakersfield, Christmas Day, 1985"

Spry: "Some Good Thing May Yet Happen"

Storyscape: "Downtown Walk, April," "You Would Not Exist," "After Ten Days in the Woods"

Sugar House Review: "Your Mother Tries to Describe Tree Blossoms," "Stodge Meadow Pond"

Superstition Review: "Losing Your Breath"

Terrain: "What Smoke Is Made Of"

Thimble Literary Magazine: "View from the Window, July"

Valparaiso Review, "Year of Drought"

Worcester Magazine: "Bargain"

For Patricia Jean Caspers

~

The way my grief will die with
me. The way it will cleave and grow
like antlers.
—Victoria Chang

Contents

What It's Important to Know

Life with Fever

Life with Fever (unfinished)

In fevered dreams life is an algebra equation
from 10th grade math, which you failed.
You try to unknot each intricate tangle of it:
$a^2 + b^2 = c^2$
where a equals the arc of the handed-down china dish,
its blue pattern of birds flying from your hand,
suddenly shattered on the kitchen floor.
And b is the first initial of a good therapist across town.
And c—What is c?
This is where your synapses hesitate, misfire,
or the tiny speed bump stalls the car
that travels the complex circuitry of your brain.
Is c the cry you held in, collected and throbbing
at the unforgiving base of your skull?
Or is c for Christ, whom you left standing on Nana's porch
the night she let go your name?
Alternately, if b is the broken bluebird mosaic, perhaps
c is the cut finger and the crimson-stained broom handle
as you swept the night's anger into the dustbin.

Then morning comes for real, damp and thirsty,
a math teacher tapping your desk.
But the answer is still locked inside its cell—
Wait, you say.
Let me begin again

Slaughtering Days

1.

Remembering is soaked with the scent of sunlight and soil,
swollen grapes and magnolias, the gargled chatter of chickens.

I walked the path from the porch to the goat pen,
watched the parade of ants cross the grape vines and sang,
Mine eyes have seen the glory of the coming of the Lord.

Stopped halfway to watch the cow roped to the fence.

Dad and Uncle Mike stood by the live oak tree,
laughed secrets to each other, held their slender guns.

Dad stood back while Uncle Mike
aimed his rifle at the cow and fired.

I must have covered my ears then.

The cow stood there as big as the entire farm.
Stubborn, Dad said. Uncle Mike shot again.

The cow knelt prayer-like on front legs;
back legs folded under slowly.
She rolled to one side
like a child under her night-quilt.

I ran all the way back to the house
to tell Nana it was done.

2.

The house always smelled of dachshund.
In the kitchen, a pig's head,
eyes covered with cotton,
bled its life into a salad bowl.

Each woman stood in a corner
with a pig quarter, a knife, and cigarette.
Nana Ivy directed the carving with her skeleton fingers.

In the next room Bob Barker shouted the bids
while Papa watched from his fireplace recliner
and Dad popped wheelies in circles
in Papa's wheelchair.

Uncle Mike hosed his boots outside,
but later he would pull me into the kitchen,
uncover the eyes of that pig, and make us
stare each other down.

Census, 1976

My nana called him Jimmy; Papa James
a formal gift, a priestly wafer pressed
onto my toddler tongue, a spell, a name
for me alone to speak, a special trust

that school day afternoons I'd find him idling
curbside bus stop, engine singing welcome
home, but first the back roads, Gotto's aisles,
the berry pocket pies, the postal bell

and druggist. Finally, our cozy chairs
between the hearth and crackling TV set
where Nana greeted us with cherry milk,
a dachshund puppy, Papa's cigarettes.

He called me pretty baby, smartest girl,
his Top Cat; Nana, polecat, both of us
his favorite patricias, ghostly pearls.
The memory of him now, nearly dust.

Blunt jackhammer, my father once said—*knife
mouth, callous brute. He loved you more than life.*

The Sewing Machine

It hides in its scratched cabinet like an ivory treasure, and I am the thief. I pull open the lid, fold it over slowly, push in the latch and pull back the secret board. I have to reach in with both hands to pull out the weight of the thing, as if delivering a reluctant baby. The strong scent of you, Nana—coffee, cigarettes, and Bay Rum—rises with it. As I sit down to sew, I hear your voice guiding me, *It's like driving a car; the pins are lines to follow. Not too fast, Nana Ivy sewed right through her finger, bone and all.* As a girl I imagined the bobbin a worried mouse running in circles, and Nana always spun him with the brightest thread. Now as I sew, my lines still crooked, I fall into the musical chug chug of the needle like the sound of the distant train we all heard the bright morning we buried her.

Earl the Pig

Aunt Sue kept the runt in her shaded trailer in Nana's back yard, called him Earl, dressed him in hand-knitted sweaters, and fed him scraps from her plate while he perched in her lap. She said he was smarter than any dachshund. When my own dachshund, Nana's gift, was killed by gas station boys, Aunt Sue said God loved him was all, wanted him close. She wouldn't eat flour, only sugar and meat, and always put too much E in my name. I took offense. Nana's funeral was the last time I saw Aunt Sue. She said, "Your nana could balance a Coors on her ass just like that." I said, "God's a selfish bastard." No, I didn't. I thought it, though, and about how the soft word, *atheist,* also had a lot of E in it. Last I heard, Aunt Sue severed her pinky toe with a fat can of stewed tomatoes. I don't know what happened to Earl, but I suspect she candied him.

Bird Damage / Fire Blight

Placer County, California

In each parcel of backyard crabgrass,

scorched soil, ant trails, star

thistle, goat thistle, goosegrass,

a lone loquat leans at the perimeter,

deep river-green leaves grin

at wild oats and mallow.

Higher fronds, paler green, arch

their backs toward winter warmth,

bursting panicles of wooly buds that soak light.

Some say freshwater carp will swim

below a loquat's branches, swallow

the orange thumbfruit, grow scales of armor,

barbelfire, turn dragon fierce, but the amber

stone, bright and wet as a pony's eye,

curdles to poison in the belly of any human.

Unlike us, the loquat flourishes

after severe pruning and no more water

than the sky's daily offering, or lack.

My father called them kumquats—

one of his smaller mistakes—

made weapons of the unripened.

From my window I watch jays thrash
the branches, gash the flesh, steal away
into farther scrub oaks. Their hunger
and late-season rain will spoil a crop,
but around here no one much cares.
The loquat, like an apricot, makes fine
jam, liqueur, pies, balsamic reduction.
Scrape and steep the leaves, sip the tea,
make a poultice for the most tender places.
Instead, I drag a ladder along uneven ground,
scatter squirrels, bees, twist the fruit
from its rough stem, fill my mouth
with the furred skin. All of my childhood
was this: gorging on neglect, praying
for my eyes to glow golden, for the smoke
to tendril from these famished lips.

Public Radio

for Ira

At thirteen every day was a slow, hot, breath
released into a windless sky.
A smear of lip gloss, hippo tongue pink,
to distract from teeth already lost to asphalt.

I stretched cotton white shorts over new hips
and flip-flopped to the gas station patio
where I swung my legs from a bench
in hopes that some traveling smoker
might offer me a Pepsi or a Kit Kat, or a ride.

I walked a rolling stretch of dead end
roads and wondered about the faces
behind windshields
whether they ate dinner together around a table,
whether they would know me.

When I should have been asleep,
I clicked on my birthday boom box, volume low,
and ballooned the empty shadows with sound.

Once I twisted the dial far into the left desert
and for the first time heard a pledge drive, felt
the down-deep body thrill of a man's rough
voice in my ear, in the dark, whispering *please.*

Problem Solving

Gary made pies on the back
of my homework page and divided
each one with his pencil, *this is two halves,*
this is four quarters.
We sat at the kitchen table
while Mom scrubbed dinner pots.

If she would only apply herself,
said Mr. Rath, and I imagined
myself a bottle of silver nail polish
in the medicine chest, and another me
leaving the color unused, closing the cabinet door.

Gary took off his union cap, scratched his head,
turned the page over, explained
the problem again.

I knew what it meant to multiply—
how cancer cells multiplied
at a dangerous rate,
subtracting life.

And what it meant to divide
one family into thirds, add
the larger fraction of another family,
how it never made one whole.

Gary was still talking about
dollars and quarters now. He pulled
a buck from his wallet, laid it
on the table. I laid my head there, too.

Got it? he asked.
His eyes were light blue,
and I could see in them why
my mom loved him, and how
he wanted me to understand
because he was work-tired
and hadn't yet showered
and because he didn't want me
to fail the fifth grade.

Yeah, I lied, *I got it now.*
But secretly I thought it must take
some kind of magic I didn't possess
to change pies into dollars
into numbers on a math sheet, turn growth
into death, to break a family,
to hold it together.

Dead Letters

~for Gary and his brother, Dale, 3/13/49–7/3/69

1.

I'm searching for info concerning my uncle who was killed in Nov.
1967 in 'Nam. I know nothing of him. He died before I was born.

2.

That hot needle was meant for men,
ink for the looping names of girls,
and not our own unmuscled arms.
The ol' man, he said—
in case I find you dead, can't see your eyes—
I know you've thought it,
but no tattoo is a promise of war.
We were scar proud.

3.

I'm looking for Shawn McCall. Last time I saw him was Nov. 9th 1970,
when he was put in a dustoff and flew into darkness.
I would really like to hear from you Shawn.
That was the worst night of my life.

4.

You loved my Gibson,
but I wouldn't let you lead.
The band needed a drummer.
We all heard you strumming unplugged
nights in the garage.

You came home suited up after practice
found strings scattered,
wood stripped,
and you wanted to fight,
just missed my head with your helmet.
Mom ran, shouting up the stairs.

Your eyes were red-ringed like that time you had the fever.
The only time I've seen you cry.

In Pleiku I told Little Tom
if I get outta here I'm fixin'
that guitar up real pretty, original gold,

and I'm giving it to my brother back home.
Little Tom, he shook his head and said, *when*.

5.

I am in desperate need to find anyone who might know of events
that occurred in Pleiku between '66 and '67. My memory is very bad.
Here is what I can put together: An ammo dump was blown up
near Bồng Sơn. There was a battle that resulted in me
(a laundry specialist) being put on morgue duty . . .

6.

I know the lie you told Mom.

7.

I was in the razorbacks (120th aviation). My nickname was Birdie.
Our slogan and banners: Death is our business. Business is good.

8.

After they boxed me home,
Mom wore her best black dress
and told them to keep the Goddamn flag
(one time she ever swore).
The Marines wouldn't take you
and how you fought them,
I know that too. I've seen you on Memorial Day
drink regret and sleep with your pistol.

Who would you have killed for me?
Somebody else's brother.

9.

I'm the son of Willard Skaggs, Jr., KIA 3-2-68. I would like to speak
with anyone who may have information about my dad.
People like you are my heroes. May you all go to heaven
because I know you have already been to hell.

10.

I saw what you did,
took you thirty years to find that Gibson in the closet—
smartest gold I've ever seen—
You keep it bro'. Play lead.

11.

*My brother was a chaplain in Vietnam. He would like to locate
the wife of Capt. Troy Oliver, C.O. of Fox Co. Oliver was killed
in action, and my brother would like to give his wife a message.*

12.

You remember Frankie Norris?
Fought with the coach every game,
spit in his face at half-time,
kicked off the team.

He went to 'Nam in '68,
came back from Quảng Trị and swore
never to live another angry day.
You ask him.

Your Mother Tries to Describe Tree Blossoms

In her neighbor's pasture, how she can see
them in the gully below as she and her dog, Frankie,
step from the red clay of the ditch tender's trail
into the narrow bend toward home.

All week she tries to tell about the white blossoms—
apricot, apple, or plum, she's uncertain—
and also about the sniper on trial, or the sniper
who was killed, but you weren't listening.
You turned off the radio and the TV, too,
because some weeks call for that kind of silence.

Now driving your mother where the two-lane road
cuts through blue oak savannah, the fields green despite winter,
despite drought. She quiets the music to talk of the soldiers,
a wolf—legend—and the actor with his quick bulk.

She wonders at the nature of the brain, of a man with a gun,
good and evil, and you have something to tell her
just as you pass that pasture, the gully, the tree with petals
like white votives flickering the dusk.
What was it you were going to say?

The Bully Tree

Your carpenter grandfather
curls in on himself
Christmas eve
like an underwatered
poinsettia,
nearly as red.
He settles
in his oversized rocker
to rummage through the luggage
of his Grandfield boyhood.
After school
he walked home
with another boy, he says.
Here he uses a slur
that I will not.
I think *He doesn't know better*.
Is this how all white people
forgive each other?
Could this story be merry?
At the corner, your grandfather
shoved the boy
to the dirt, buried
white hands
deep in pockets
that weren't his, scooped
the jingling coins and ran.
You chuckle then.
Does the thieved man
tell his grandchildren, too,
how he hit dirt?
Did he curse?
I hear this story

and know you better,
stepbrother,
but I don't like us any more.

After Ten Days in the Woods

1.

That night the old friend you feared
tapped politely at the cabin window,
like a crane fly begging for light.

You opened the glass to welcome him,
offered tea from your own cup, cut the stitches
loose from your chest and let him home.

He stretched long into the shape of your body,
and the mourning began.

2.

Morning thundered you from the dream
of your brother in his blue flannel shirt,
young and red-eyed; he's been gone so long.

Outside, hunters shot waterfowl in the autumn air.
Their fire hammered the forest, and you wept
for each victory, death's free fall, the dog's chase.

The sky, funeral dark. How long can this last?
You pillowed your head and slept again.

3.

The storm shouted itself hoarse by dusk,
and the singing frogs called you to rise slowly
against the sting-eyed wind to Cattail Pond

and the rainsoaked pasture where you sat quietly
with the broken bones of aspen and alder,
and asked for respite from this familiar burden.

And there, suddenly before you, was the copse
of burnt-yellow maple, and a single spindle tree blooming
obscenely pink, while summer lay tattered at its roots.

Saint Vitus's Dance

for my mother

Say trinucleotide.
Imagine bioluminescence
glittering in the sea of our genes,
the moonlight of the skull.
Why not make it beautiful?
If, like the tide, its repetition
is endless, call this chain a quadrille,
see how our family dances?

And here's Saint Vitus, freshly Christian.
Watch him drift above himself,
swim along the current of prayer
as the emperor's servants touch fire
to the pyre, as the water simmers,
and the marrow of him turns feverful.

Vitus pressed his hands upon
so many jittered bodies, healed them,
and the rulers boiled him anyway.
Can we blame him if he turns
away from our ballroom?
He's tired now, and just a boy.

Pacific Tide Pools, July

Before divorce anchored Grandma to broken trailer windows.

Before Grandma's boyfriend took the girl cousins for a long ride

    in the country.

Before no one believed what happened there.

Before Grandpa gave up the swing shift.

Before he traded Olympia for Shasta.

Before he told Mom her birth secret.

Before Huntington's stalked us one-by-one.

Before it silenced Grandma.

Before it silenced our aunts.

Grandpa drove the camper to Bodega Bay

where my cuffed jeans filled with ocean sting.

Nights I carried the beach with me,

snuggled between my grandparents' warm backs in the camp bed.

Mornings Grandpa, laughing, complained about the scratchy sand

    in his boxers

while Grandma snapped sheets in the wind.

After I Discover My Dutch Grandfather Is Not My Biological Grandfather, He Offers Me Tulips Instead: An Erasure

all the world went mad. a sailor mistook

a flame-like white and red petal—it grew

speculation exploded into ruin

for decades, a warning about the perils of absurdity

none of these stories are true

what really happened and how

she dug, always joke

people are so interested in this incident

because they think they can draw lessons:

at the border, so many flowers.

the mother bulb flowering; the next year broken

the effect was unpredictable: a gamble, bizarre

after all.

the rage to possess so great,

neglect promised

at least that's what has always been claimed

fact, a much harder thing

everything about the story is wrong:

trust was really no mechanism

but it didn't cause the collapse,

an innocent sailor wading in hope, insistence,

stayed with us to this day

god punishes pride

she didn't set out to stumble upon the truth

Unfinished Abecedarian of DNA

Another ancestor revealed:
Brothers and sisters of your mother
Cousins as an undiscovered constellation
Desert of language between decades
Every living relative now a question:
Faith. What makes a man
Grandfather?
How many lost granddaughters?
Imagine a family woven as strong as the line where the laundry
    was strung
Just beyond the vegetable patch where Grandma worked mornings
    alone. This
Kind of family doesn't fly like a worn blouse in the gust of an
    oncoming storm.
Let every geranium in her flowerbed blossom again, though she
    lied about the
Meatloaf packed in his lunch, and
Names she gave us—
O, Mother, what will they call us now?

La Historia: Juera

I whittle your life, Agapita Cervantes,
from ink stamps, history books, photographs
as brittle as the wings of a sun-bleached fly.

I trace your path, as you crossed yourself,
the border, crossed and crossed again,
a baste stitch needling the seam as quickly
as war tore at the threads.

Was it meant to be fleeting?

That Wyoming July you broke
from the white blood
of sugar beets, bore down
and birthed my grandfather,
mi familia encubierta.

Was homesickness the mew of an orphan kitten,
chasing your heels from sow to harvest?

Perhaps you were whip-tongued,
a revolution all your own.

If I have only this,
let me imagine us here in porch sunlight
where our chisels glint and the balsa wood takes shape.

Do you claim me, I ask,
if my eyes, my skin, my words are all wrong?

Cuidado, granddaughter, you say.
No te cortes.

Double Negative

I handed over *ain't* as willingly as rain-gullied snails collected
after a storm and tried to wrestle the contraction from my
cousins—*ain't* too hungry, *ain't* got no milk, *ain't* gonna eat
watered cereal again—but it anchored their tongues.

Don't want no one. I gave what *I seen,* gave my *hunnerd* pleases
and *cee-ment* heart and turned my hard, mischievous *E* to soft ash,
and then gave more: the cousins themselves with their chick fuzz
hair, our summer names spun in sparklers against the stars.

Next went their mothers; aunts with nicotine kisses and *Babys*
and *Sissys* and sunflower seed spittle in a *Pessi* can. Finally, I sent
away my siblings and their red-capped devotion, as if we had never
stomped empty Buds in burnt July grass, our bare legs splattered
with the hot foam of each crush.

I gave all of it for one discombobulated alphabet: *beleaguered,
ephemeral, insouciance*, for a carbon black tap dance across
cellulose, for my place at the front of the class where a student says
I seen, and the word is a dull *saw* that grates my throat *seen seen
seen*—who am I to topple

that domino of loss?

Family Portrait

The mother waits nights with warm casserole,

watered wine and the same record spinning

until she sleeps in the baby's room.

She catches morning insults between her teeth,

chews them with her coffee.

The sister rides her bicycle after school

until mothers call from porches, *You best get home now darlin'*.

The father bruises blue with the fruit of his hand,

salts the family with whiskey slang.

The mother gathers baby clothes from the dark apartment.

In the driveway the chubby infant sleeps in Grandma's arms.

The brother's teeth come in crooked.

He prays to Jesus for new shoes,

makes toast on school mornings,

sweats in the night silence.

Days, the father collects bar machine quarters

in a fog of alcohol and urine.

Sister kicks a single stone around the school yard,

wets her corduroy pants in the library,

waits her turn to bring red marshmallow Jell-O to class.

The father covers the floor of his dill green Cadillac

with fruit pie wrappers as he drives daily

between orchard towns and Sacramento,
whistles to himself, *Everything, gone.*

Some Flawed Magic

Father As

1.

Rooster

Golden comet, you.
Dawn-screeched, dusting the terrain.
Your wide, wide reach of blue.
Tetherless and wander-worn,
there's nowhere you can't not fly.

2.

Salesman (1960)

   Your dad could sell white blackbirds. ~ Cousin Chuck

Nana collected August peaches from the heaviest branches
made cobbler of the scabbed or lopsided harvest,
filled brown bags with the roundest, red-cheeked fruit.

She loaded my father's Murray bike basket, warned him
of the swerve, the potholes, stirring the grit. He couldn't sell
what was spilled, couldn't reach the boughs for more.

How he must have pedaled through the sweet, the yellow weight,
the possibility of bruising so much sunshine.

3.

Futurism

You were never
seawash pink dusk, hands
shouldering the babies.

You were bright, yolky tempera, shadowed city street,
wash of red, trace of kinetic rhythm
phone line silhouette in the periphery,
scratch of indiscernible pentimento.

4.

False Awakening

The night rings each dream,
and in this new wakefulness
my father wants to know where to find me.
Child-scryer, I divined the telephone
for his living patterns, found only static.
Now he watches for me, he says, at that Irish pub in Frisco,
El Faro beach, the Peppermill.
The Mill went under years ago, I say.
Lies, the voice of my ghost father laughs through the line.
You always did believe those lies.

Ode to E.B.

Once in a while something slips—one of the actors goes up in his lines and the whole performance stumbles and halts. My pig simply failed to show up for a meal.

—E.B. White

1.

I think of you in the barn dark—
for how many days?—while summer
churned itself slowly into autumn.
You're there, haloed by white-feathered
swallows' nests and propped
on a three-legged milking stool—
a bottle of castor oil,
an enema tube, and pot-bellied
doxie your only companions—
except for the pig,
whose fine-haired back you scratch
as you eye his irksome spots
and inspect his leathered ears
in the lantern light, listening
for each breath.

There, in the sawdust night,
you know you can't save him.

2.

After the farmer's burial,
after you've seen how the wind moves
the threadbare theater curtain
between each life,
you sit with your inkpot potions,
until, from the tinker and worry,
you fashion yourself an elegant spider.

51

3.

Like you, Elwyn,
I sit in my windowless room
each evening, trying my hand
at some flawed magic,
weaving another world
in which the dead
are not dead
but dancing.

How to Become Detail-Oriented

Put down your name,
the sound of it
in your father's mouth—
the grumble of an El Camino
as it races center street,
the wish of its passing
so close you could almost
touch your fingers
to the sun-strewn glass.

Put down the mud,
sweet animal
scent of the midnight
river where you stood,
a barefoot girl
slinging a starry line
to the catfish
as your father buzzed
his laughter from the rushes,
how you hoped a fish
might divulge secrets
from its depths,
how you feared
its barbel sting.

Replace the whistle,
the small locomotive
of your breath
thrumming the reeds
of a forbidden harmonica,
inhaling the silver
taste of your father's blues
between your lips.

Still the film
of the San Francisco
skyline, a cold blur
between girders,
the heartbeat
of decking
below car tires,
and beyond, the longing
distance of his last call,
a question—
is burial a kind
of forgiveness?—
the one time
you heard
your father cry.

A Gas Station Near Bakersfield, Christmas 1983

I'm locked in a bathroom
with the stink of grease and mold.
No windows.
Dad pumps gas outside.
We're six hours from home,
and he's forgotten me before.
He'll speed his El Camino down the highway,
slap his hands on the wheel,
and sing Quincy Jones, *Ai No Corrida*
all the way to Ensenada
before he remembers me.
Mom said
he just wants to buy drugs
but she let me go,
and now this steel door
won't budge.
I bang on it, give up,
sit on the toilet,
listen to engines start,
and tires crunch over glass.
Then his voice comes
so handsome through the wall,
You okay, kiddo?
I sob my answer,
and in his one heroic moment
my father hurls the bear of himself
against that door,
and sunlight
comes crashing in.

While Driving Highway 80, I Think of My Father

Past the crop of Sacramento high-rises
over the water-neglected riverbed,
stopping at a diner in Davis for fried eggs and toast.

When I was a girl you drove this highway every day.

You must have known how many trees were in that orchard,
exactly when the sun-scrubbed hills soaked to green velvet.

How many songs played between this truck stop
and the next produce stand?

One morning when I was four we drove to San Francisco—
the other side of the world—
and I flew a kite in the big park.

Last night, from across the continent, you told me
how you hate the golden state and everything in it.

I travel this highway back to where I was born
and wonder about the Carolina roads you drive now,
whether, like these, the fields have blossomed into strip malls.

Whether, from your window, you've ever seen
a flock of starlings change direction in the wind.

Double Yellow

Because one of Missy's pupils was the shape of Florida, she wore deep black sunglasses that gloved her face. She said trust is hard to come by with shaded eyes. She was driving a two-lane road out past Medicine Creek when a distant pickup drifted across the narrow asphalt. Missy, so generous, filled the gap on the other side. The pickup corrected, and then there was no gap. Surgeons stitched her body together but couldn't repair her eyes. I wonder, thirty years later, how many times she's told that story—slim rows of corn flashing by, broad sky, the tractor nuzzling grass in the far field, the wrong-sided pickup. In the driver's seat, would I have stopped altogether, swept the gravel shoulder? Maybe there was no margin, only a steep embankment to ditchwater on either side, like the canals watering the farmland where, as a girl, I swam with my father, long before he crossed his own narrow piece of Florida highway. I had never wondered about the man who stole daylight from my friend's eyes, what distracted him from his obligation to that stretch of road. Maybe he and my father both were drawn to twilight glimmering gold across the landscape, beckoning the stars one last time.

If the Swerve Was Fatal

That is: his death that day intended—fate:

    his pickup shined and sold; the wheels' etern-

        al destiny to cross the double line, the weight

        of his body's forward pitch, of our collective grief

            overwintering among stars, yellowing

    with patience for its moment—there's a question

to be answered. The riverbank is shadowed with questions,

    an October Glory letting its beauty go, late reminder—the fate

        of seasons. A bride never wears yellow.

    The June morning she answered the universe, and turned

to her groom, did she, too, feel the oncoming rush of grief,

pause in her vowtaking, weary with the weight

        of future loneliness? *Wait*

      I tell her past self. Unwind every question.

    This is not a wedding but a funeral, bliss and grief

spilled in equal proportion. Red, the color of fate,

the brilliant shade of dress I might have worn, had I turned

from sentiment, toward something true—a bouquet of yellow

anemones for a widowed bride—stranger. Sadness in yellowed

dusk arrives like a salesman at an unlocked door, the weight

of his calloused hand on the frame, turning

the ache into a bargain, his mouth full of questions.

Isn't the past always for sale? he asks, as I watch the future fade

below the horizon, fail to argue away this guest, this grief.

What if, instead, death is a series of choices—our grief

an option untaken, a little yellow

diner where my father might have sobered himself, stirred fate

into a chipped mug of coffee, the weight

of undissolved sugar on his tongue, like a question

he forgot to ask: side road, gas station, shoreline, nesting terns.

I choose my father's telephone laughter, the turn

of his voice on a punch line. I empty the flask of his grief

into the river, steal the keys, answer all the questions

      he left on my voicemail that spring morning. No yell-

ing at the disconnect, the newspaper clippings, late obits, waiting

    forgiveness from strangers whose lives continue to fade.

Thirteen autumns this maple has caught fire, returned to yellow

borne its grief through winter, branches weighted

    with unanswerable questions, heavy with frost, a bride to fate.

Mourning, with Hummingbirds

Days later, Rick and I sat on the porch,
the baby, colicky in my arms.
A blue jay tumbled behind us,
cornered on the wooden slats.

A jewel-green body made crosses above our heads,
her needle-beak a threat.

I remembered the hummingbird
in Carole Oles' poem about her children,
how fast they're gone.
I cried when I read it, only
I didn't have children then.

That same year I lay with a man
I did not yet love, listening to BB King
sing about his hummingbird.
Don't fly, he sang.

Seems all wrong to call them birds,
the word itself too heavy.

In the foothills, Grandpa Grady said,
folks shouldn't leave feeders out too late in the season
or the birds don't know it's time to go,
are taken by the frost.

We stood in Grandma's garden once—
Would you remember, Dad, if you were here? —
That mildew scent of geraniums humid around us.
A hummingbird whirred close to my head,
frightened me.

You pointed and said,
when a hummingbird stills his wings, he dies.
I was young enough to believe you.

Some Good Thing May Yet Happen

What gives dignity to death is the dignity
of the life that preceded it.
—Dr. Sherwin Nuland

The summer of sun-scorched concrete
pockmarked with chewing gum,
Dad and I sat in his El Camino
in the parking lot of his apartment complex,
two blocks from Scandia Family Fun Center
where I spent most days scouring
the universe of carpet for lost tokens.
The sweat gathered at the back of my knees,
tickled my calves on its way to my flip flops.
I was eager for the air-conditioned indoors,
but Dad needed to tell me
right there in the heat of the car:
He couldn't be my father anymore—
a friend, maybe, buddy, not Dad.
I nodded, silent.
The memory is flipped now,
a backward negative,
so that in my mind
Dad sits on the passenger side,
me, beside him, thirteen,
hands gripping the wheel.

How It's Done

Begin with tenacity, the nested feet of an emperor penguin.
Add the steady back of a giant water bug, wide and flat as an ever-
    watching eye.
Craft a rib of clay scraped from your own night-tended garden,
and above his gaze—poached from a doting dachshund—
embroider the barbuled plumage of a sand grouse, that you may
    never thirst.
In honor of your mother, pour an elixir of prairie vole love
slowly down a gullet slit from a white-throated sparrow
as he whistles to his chicks, *peabody peabody peabody.*
Fatten the belly on the milk of a male Dayak fruit bat:
Here is where you will affix the patient pouch of a seahorse.
To the torso, stitch the plush arms of an owl monkey—
that you may always be held—and if the primate
flashes his lantern eyes at the loss,
explain the cruel but necessary logic, theorems scratched
and scratched again in childhood notebooks.
Finally, here's the magic, and it's your best trick:
The heart you thrust behind the carved breastbone
of this flawless father, must be
as tender as a wren, pulsing warmly, and plucked
from your own severed chest.

Bargain

What I want is an autumn parade
a smackdab November hoopla,
marching bands jazz dancing "It Don't Mean a Thing"
up Park Avenue while clowns
cartwheel through harvest leaves
and unicyclers toss candy already
melting in the dusty rain.
I want confetti and me
atop a fairytale pink frosted cake,
my tiara at a jaunty angle, my hands
kiss-waving at you
the only bystander, fluttering
your Happy Birthday flag
in the dry California wind.
What I want is my name
trailed behind airplanes
in sparkly fuchsia letters, big as sunshine
against the overcast slow-
swagger-toward-winter sky.
And after, I want a surprise soiree
where fountains pee ginger ale and waiters
in black jackets carry crudités and tapenade
and all the people I love cheer
when you play solo harmonica
in the ballad you've written just for me.
I want to go back to plump-with-summer June,
take the driver's seat, take the stash from your pocket.
I want you alive.
I want this to be the year
you call on the anniversary of my birth
and say *I remembered.*

Downtown Walk, April

The baby pulls your hair and pats your shoulders
from his backpack. You whinny, neigh,
and gallop him to sleep for the mile walk,
his head resting in the valley of your spine.
The trees on Central Avenue leaf themselves the palest green
while white petals gather in the gutter like snow.
A college couple sit on a stoop and trade kisses
in their morning blanket.
By the time you reach Park Street, you are nineteen
again, and the baby a sack of worn books,
thumbed fat and finger-stained.
Nineteen and your dad is alive, and though you don't speak,
time is still a puppy leashed to a parking meter
who yaps and wags her greeting.
The coffee shop bell jingles and you order the usual
from the lip-pierced barista who remembers your name.
Now there's a hot cup in one hand as you wander
bookshelves, loll and sip, read magazine after
lazy magazine, listen to the bookworkers chatter
about *Catcher in the Rye* until you stumble over
Kooser's poem about death's pre-dawn call.
You read it twice before the journal pages are wet,
remembering Chuck's words, *I got some bad news, Darlin'*.
The baby stirs, kicks your haunches with both heels.

風の電話

When Itaru Sasaki lost his cousin in 2010, he decided to build a glass-paneled phone booth in his hilltop garden with a disconnected rotary phone inside for communicating with his lost relative.

—Atlas Obscura

The bereft roam the hillside,
carry grief like a hollow bowl,
never empty, never full. They wander
against the September glare
or hush through January snow.

I wonder myself there
in your anniversary days, the cusp
of solstice, the sense of the door you closed
so close, perpetually the moment
between fracture and howl.

Unlatching the glass box, I whisper
inside, stand on the bracings of time,
the cool of the receiver against my ear.
Are you there?

Are you anywhere
without the ballast of bones?
With the ash of your ears,
what do you make of these words
tossed like stones into the wind?

Take them, father.
Build a cairn
so that one day I may find my way home.

What It's Important to Know

You Would Not Exist

If I had eaten dinner
If he had not ordered tequila
If Philip Levine had not been invited to read
If your father had not caught up with me in the hallway,
If he had not asked, If I had not said yes,
said no, my boyfriend is waiting in his truck outside
If the boyfriend had not had a meeting
If Levine had not mentioned the apple of his eye
If I had not been the apple of my grandfather's eye
If your father had not opened a Nalgene bottle full of black licorice,
and peeled an orange, there in the auditorium dark where we floated,
reeking of Cuervo and the fruit on our hands
If he had not ordered Russian apples in the bar, later,
toasted my grandfather, and argued some inane point to silence
If he had not brought me an apple, large and deep red,
waiting by the bike racks while students ran to class
and bells clanged
If we had not ditched English, ridden our bikes
through Bidwell, rested under an oak
If I had not, nervous talking, brought out my fervor
for the Spanish words *fuego, incendio*—blaze, arson—
If he had not asked *Which fire are you?*

Bowline

for O~

Your father kept a piece of blue cord in his pocket

like the one wrapped around

the small, red pears of your feet

when you wailed into the world.

He knotted and burned the pocket cord

with a gas station lighter,

and slipped it on my wedding finger.

It wasn't because

you were growing there, he said,

a swell under the sleeping bag, under the searching

gaze of the lighthouse lantern.

In defiance you look so like him,

when you blame me for the way I love

everyone too soon.

Your father said exactly that

in the days that were supposed

to be saltwater sweet. I should have jumped

on my bicycle, kept pedaling,

would have, maybe, but I sensed you

there already, unfolding your cells

in the mystery, and I wanted you

to know him, to see how his lips

quiver in nervousness, like that night
when he said the knot would unravel,
fall away, not to mistake its loosening
for something we'd lost.

Chico, September

Your father and I spent our summer money
renting the fuchsia two-room apartment,
unboxed Miles Davis and Shakespeare,
sold the rest for thirty grocery dollars,
searched the paper every morning.

After our written request for food stamps,
I was sent to the clinic for bloodproof
on the wrong day, and wandered
between bewildered and paper-faced girls.
They wore dark sweat-pants,
held their mother's hands.

The backroom nurses were quietly distracted.
I waited a long time and carried
my own vial of urine. One nurse
sat with me, finally.
You're four months now.
We have late terminations. You'll have
to come in soon though—next week.
My breath slipped.
I offered my welfare papers, said, *No thank you,*
sweet, as if declining milk in my tea.

What Smoke Is Made Of

Paradise, California, 1997

In the particle dark, we rose like mist.
We mattered.

The door of dawn unlatched,
and we trumbled our clothes on in its shine.
His belt clinked against itself like a clock.

Our footsteps stirred the damp scent of soil
as the pickup doors creaked open,
and I lumbered my roundness into the rectangle of space.

We raced the ridge in the morning quiet,
chasing sunlight, hours before
she arrived with her raspy squall, cradle cap,
boxer's fists, and everything

everything that we were combusted,
leaving only the vapor of that moment,
as we watched the sun churn
the clouds above the valley, and held fast
to the horizon, named it something like a vow.

Canyon Fire

Another August morning the sky opens
its smoke-heavy wings, and after so many years of silence,
we hello each other in the cafe,
as if not knowing the wooded place
where we parked my hatchback
all those other harvest nights is blistering, thick with ash—
gone—the hideaway where we kissed ourselves dry,
kissed until we slept with our names in our mouths.

While the barista writes my name on a paper cup with a wink,
the news rack shouts a tally of blackened acreage, numbers
of injured firefighters, the impossible terrain, the dearth of rain,
we stumble our way through smogged skylines,
school cancellations, containment,
and if I stay too long I might tell you
I dreamed the dream again.

It's autumn and you ask to drive away from that night forest,
from the constancy of evergreens, and I say *yes,*
though our feet are as bare as our pockets,
yes, though your parents are waiting up.

We drive the rough vein of the valley

and arrive at the ocean with the dawn gulls.

We roll our pant legs, wade into the cold Pacific,

christened by our own salt and desire, and the knowledge

that one day you will be a man who runs long treks

of forgetting through the tangle of manzanita, madrone,

sugar pine and doesn't dream of the sea at all.

View from the Window, July

Again our children run the dock—
clatter, thunk, splash.

I watch from the house,
unpack boxes, hang my western life

on New England walls,
fold myself into pine drawers.

There's a flash of bright swimsuit
through a maze of green-leafed oaks,

the dash and leap, like an Olympic
long jumper, as far

as speed, thrust, and body allow.

Just before fear grabs their ankles,
they fling themselves over the threshold,

and shriek with falling joy.

Postcard from the Winterside of Spring

for J~

The lake is an icy half moon
water eclipses each day.

The geese, black questions
on the far pond bank,

honk disapproval
at the bird dog's tendu.

Your father
sloshes a labyrinth
of snow melt

sun wishing, crocus
anxious, robin
ready.

Write soon.

There is no summer
without you.

Stodge Meadow Pond

His whittled tongue so sharp and lizard blue,
our British son arrives unsunned and clock-
shy, dusking summer pondside. Winter boots
unwieldy comfort, shock of water's balk.

Our daughter bunkers up in bed all hours,
deciphers currents, fevered notes that she
has written self-to-self. Unknocking doors,
unshelving stars, her mood is mystery.

The naiads crack their homes, those gray and fright-
ful tanks, convulse, shed their armor, burst
cerulean, all shimmer, arrowed light.
Abandoned husks: forgotten, crumpled curses.

Now stow the oars, love, drift beyond the rise—
let's learn to hum the waltz of dragonflies.

Year of Drought

At the pond's edge, waterside of blueberries,
a frenzy of mullet tumbles,
and water swirls silver flashes.

No snow pack this year
to bring the stream from the mountain,
wash last season's sorrow over the spillway.

Bereft of swift water, a place to spawn,
the mullet twist and writhe in shallows,
disbelief in suspense.

While the fish turn in dreams
of other springs, the blue heron hunkers,
fills his belly with their want.

Husband, I don't know how to tell you
I want to go home.

My Husband Reads *Life of Pi* Aloud While We Await a Second External Cephalic Version

The hospital room is a sea at play,
four walls of overcast sky.

The bed, an old sloop, and you a stowaway
curled tight inside the life raft of my belly.

For days we've drifted, offered dry rations,
sung from the gunwales:

"Come out, come out, whoever you are."
You stay in your capsized dream.

Albuterol drips like rain
as waves tip and lurch the hull—

Is that the skitter and plunge
of a heart? Yours or mine?

I promise there will always be hyenas
as the heart monitor whoops,

stalks the flat line of its prey.
One day I will be the orangutan,

and, sure, all of the world is an island
that devours humans, spits our teeth into the heavens.

Let's swim to shore anyway, little nautilus, reluctant mariner.
There are so many stories to tell.

Losing Your Breath

for Seamus, atheist, age 7~

It isn't something you misplace
like a piece of bulldozer puzzle
slipped into the pocket of a too-small
winter coat, donated and forgotten.

You wake in the night and try to capture the air,
some sort of July firefly you can't swoop
into the mason jars of your lungs.

But your lungs are not glass;
they're tissue and muscle and cartilage,
300 million capillaries, waiting
for that old magic trick of oxygen.

The night we raced through the campground,
winding fast down pine-lined roads, the sky,
black before us, was no comfort
with its bright spectacle of constellations.

Each wheezed breath became our rosary
as your dad carried you
across the empty hospital parking lot,

and I thought then about the small mystery
inside of you, struggling to hold onto this life,
to this body-machine.

It's everything I know of god.

The Narcissus Bulb

Before his birth, I had never seen
a penis wrapped in foreskin like a small, unblossomed bulb.

I bathed and diapered him, and together, after a time,
we aimed his miniature elephant's trunk
and its unreliable spout, as if I were a practiced mentor.

There's no scribbled date in the baby book
to note his last unabashed slosh in tub bubbles,
while I rested ringside and sang—

Mother Duck said quack quack quack.

At eleven, my son asks me to leave him alone
with the doctor, and I listen
to his murmured answers through the door.

At night I dream my hand
where it no longer belongs.

There is the possibility
of too much mother love.

But once, his boy body
was my body, and mine
an archway of bone where he huddled,
warmed for a season,
by my blood.

Portrait of a Son as Babyface

When life puts you in tough situations, don't say, "why me?"
Just say, "try me."

—Dwayne Johnson

Your son is braced to body slam—he roars:
No tale of woodland knight, no cup of dice,
cartoon, warm slice of pie, or plane in flight
will shift his torso's quick trajectory.

Your tender caring fills him now, the way
colostrum filled his infant belly sweet.
One areola cactus, one petite
O, robin-open, turtle-mouth—and say

that swaddling was a holy kind of—POW!—
So make a gift: your best sharpshooter.
Not long 'til boyhood is his jobber, or
he turns where mothers cannot go, but know:

Inside of him is everything you are—
CRASH!—swiftly squashing you against the floor.

Re-Reading the Pregnancy Book Twenty Years Later

Every day more rain

while I imagined you burclover,

starry points hitched and unspooling

in the mystery of my body.

"What It's Important to Know"

each chapter of the baby manual read,

and nightly I tripped on the riddle again,

unwilling to step into the urgency.

What is important to know?

A mother alligator will crack the shell

of her hatchling just so

and in the damp cavern of her jaws

carry her glimmering slip of reptile tenderly

to the water's edge.

What is it important to know?

Your father brought violets in a plain clay pot,

and they tumbled over the banister,

smashed on gravel two stories below.

The violence in the breaking.

What's important to know?

A dolphin will grieve her lost calf,

abide hunger to carry its small weight

alone through blue fields of water.

Salt into salt.

It's important that you know

I devoured the pages with bags of dried WIC beans

and jars of peanut butter, one leap beyond

where the words said I'd find you—

pink salamander, hairless kitten.

You stole away with my sleep, my breath.

What's important?

I created you, little sister,

early daughter,

out of my own sweat and milk.

Your absence is my absence.

This is not grief,

but its sister perhaps,

the goodbye of growing up.

Notes:

"Dead Letters": The italicized stanzas of this poem were found in online postings at a now defunct website for veterans of the Vietnam war and their family members.

"After I Discover My Grandfather Is Not My Biological Grandfather, He Offers Me Tulips Instead: An Erasure": All text found in "There Never Was a Real Tulip Fever" by Lorraine Boissoneault at *Smithsonian Magazine*.

About the Author

Patricia Caspers is an award-winning poet, journalist, and columnist. Her first book, *In the Belly of the Albatross*, was published by Glass Lyre Press in 2015. She earned an MFA in creative writing from Mills College, and she is the founding / managing editor of *West Trestle Review.* She lives with her family in the foothills of northern California.

www.ingramcontent.com/pod-product-compliance
Lightning Source LLC
Chambersburg PA
CBHW020313090426

42735CB00009B/1322